VENETIA RUMBOLD

My Life

Copyright © 2013 Venetia Rumbold
Find out more about the author by visiting
zestauthors.com/mylife

Published by Zest Publishing
Ternion Court, 264-268 Upper Fourth Street,
Milton Keynes, MK9 1DP, United Kingdom
www.zestpublishing.com

British Library Cataloguing in Publication Data
A catalogue record is available from the British Library
ISBN 978-0-9574502-1-9

Printed and bound in Great Britain and
Distributed Internationally by the Ingram Content
Group

Cover Design and Typeset by Art Innovations, India
Set in Garamond

I wish to thank and acknowledge Barbara Smith, Mariette Louw, Dorothy Rose, and Sarah Clarkson for their help in writing this book.

CONTENTS

Introduction

*They shall eagerly utter the memory of Your
abundant goodness, and will shout joyfully of Your
Righteousness.*

-Psalm 145:7

That which inspired me to write the highlights of my life, and of my walk with the Lord, was the desire to make known the goodness, the faithfulness, and the amazing love of the Lord for me. He loves all of His children with a truly personal love, and treats us as if we were the only one in the world. We are His handiwork, and though we all have our ups and downs in life, "we know that God causes all things to work together for good to those who love God, to those who are called according to His purpose." (Romans 8:28)

I trust that my testimony will encourage any who struggle in any way with their self-worth. As long as our lives have been surrendered to Him, it does not matter where we are, for He has a destiny for each one of us, and there is no need for us to try to be like anyone else. In His love, we are all unique.

Venetia Rumbold

My Childhood

I was born on December 8th, 1941, to a British diplomatic family residing in Washington D.C. We sailed to England when I was only eleven months old, and my older sister Serena was two. The voyage was made on a ship in a wartime convoy; I am thankful I was only a baby and ignorant of all that was going on in the world. My younger sister Camilla was born on the 17th of August 1943, and my brother Henry on the 24th of December, 1947.

Because my father, Sir Anthony Rumbold, was a diplomat, his posting changed every three years, and this resulted in our moving house a lot. As a child, I experienced life in London, Prague, the Avon valley in Wiltshire, and many other places. My Father came from a line of diplomats. His father (my grandfather), Sir Horace Rumbold, had been the British Ambassador in Berlin at the time of the rise of Hitler in the thirties. My mother, Felicity, was the daughter of Lt. Col. Frederick Bailey, and the Lady Janet Bailey, who was the second daughter of the first Earl of Inchcape of Glennap Castle, Ayrshire. My paternal grandfather died in 1941 before I was born, and my other grandfather, Lt. Col. Frederick Bailey died in 1951. For as long as I can remember, my maternal grandparents resided at Lake House, in Lake, a village in the Avon valley in Wiltshire. In her widowhood, my other grandmother resided for a time in a grace and favour house at Kew Gardens, so my grandmothers were known as "Granny at Kew," and "Granny at Lake."

The culture I was brought up in is vastly different from the culture in which I have lived since I left home at the age of nineteen. Looking back to my grandparent's generation, it looks to me like the final chapter in the period of the feudal society, or the upstairs and downstairs era. My mother had three brothers and one sister, and in the early days of their upbringing, they were cared for by nannies and governesses. To see their mother, they had to put on their best clothes and go down to tea. Children in that time were to be seen but not heard.

In my childhood there were still many servants at Lake House and the ones I remember best are Mr. and Mrs. Hull and Jessie. Mr. Hull was the chauffeur and the butler, and Mrs. Hull was the cook. Jessie was my grandmother's personal maid, and she always addressed her as "my lady." My grandmother was a widow for many years. I do not remember my grandfather well, but I can remember a portrait of him where he is carrying a gun. My grandfather would invite guests to participate in shoots during which they would hunt game on the estate. Apart from the servants I have mentioned, there would have been a gamekeeper, farm labourers, gardeners, and various others. I was told that before my time, my grandparent's employed footmen as well.

There were times when we stayed at Lake. At weekends there were often guests, and when the house was full and guests were invited to stay for lunch or dinner, the large dining room would be used. I can especially remember breakfasts when we sat at the long dining room table on which there would be gleaming silver coffee pots. To this day, I can still remember the taste of that coffee.

Everything that I have written about to this point comes from what I have been told about my family background, and from my own childhood memories starting at the age of fourteen. Who knows when a child begins to remember events that have occurred in their lives, to recall the scenery of their home and the surrounding area in which they grew up? Most people, when they reach adulthood, can look back on their childhood and remember their victories and failures, joys and sorrows, and recollect all that they have learned. For me, things were a little different. It was as if I'd been born already in my teens.

I was a healthy child until I suddenly developed encephalitis (inflammation of the brain) at the age of eight. This illness caused me to suffer major convulsions together with a total loss of memory. I needed intense care at this time, and no one can count the many hours of unconsciousness I suffered during this sickness. The result of the illness was that it erased from my mind all memories of my life before I became ill. I could not remember anything and had difficulty learning anything new. I am glad that I cannot remember the years of suffering, but I would like to remember the years before.

In the fifties, my parents bought a Jacobean Manor House called "Hatch House" with a large estate. This estate is situated in Wiltshire on the edge of Dorset. The nearest big shopping town is Salisbury, which is famous for its cathedral. At Hatch, my parents employed a cook, maids, and a butler named "Mr Kenyon," gardeners, farm labourers, and others. As children, my siblings and I were not allowed in the kitchen, so we did not learn to cook before we left home. We had ponies though, so we went out riding. On the farm there was a large herd of Guernsey cows, and delicious, yellow, creamy milk was brought up to the house in a milk churn. The milk was never purified, but we never got sick. At Hatch House, just as at Lake, children were to be seen and not heard. But there

Venetia's Childhood Home

is one thing I greatly appreciated in my childhood, which was the freedom we had to play. We were given so much open space. With the gardens, woods, and countryside open to us, we wandered, explored, and climbed trees. The health and safety authorities did not interfere, or limit our freedom.

During the early years of our upbringing we were cared for by nannies, and my brother Henry had a governess during the time my father held a post in Paris. My mother used to take us all to the local Anglican Church. We each had our own Bible, and we were taught to say our prayers before going to bed. In the nursery there was a good supply of books, including Bible stories. As well as the stories about Jesus and His miracles, my favourite stories were of Daniel in the den of lions, of Shadrach, Meshach, and Abed-nego in the fiery furnace, Moses in the bulrushes, and Samson. I believed every Bible story that I read. In fact, it never occurred to me not to believe.

As children, my siblings and I were all sent to boarding schools, so that we were only at home during the school holidays. We did not have a close relationship with our parents, although as adults, we have all appreciated that they cared for us to the best of their understanding. My mother had received so little love and affection in her own upbringing that she did not have the knowledge or even the understanding of the need that every child has for love and affection. You truly cannot replace love and affection with material things.

When my father came down to breakfast he would sit at the table and read the newspaper. It was hard to talk to him. He was very much caught up in the world of diplomacy. At the time of our move to Hatch House, my father was secretary for Sir Anthony Eden, and later on, for Harold Macmillan. At the end of his career he was the British ambassador in Bangkok, and then in Vienna.

As I have said, we were only at home during the school holidays. I have been told that when I was twelve, I was sent to a special centre called "Hengrove" in St. Leonard's, near Tring, Hertfordshire. During my time there, I missed out on a summer holiday when my family went to Mont St. Michelle. I remember the address of this centre because there was a post card that sat on the mantle piece in our nursery for many years, with a photo of Mont St. Michelle, addressed to me at Hengrove. I was taken out of this institution after a year, because during my time there, my illness continued to worsen. I was then sent to another boarding school called "Zeals House" which was nearer to home.

One day when I was fourteen, and staying at Zeals House, my mother informed me that she would be taking me to visit the Reverend Gordon Sharp, the vicar in a small village in Dorset, to receive the laying on of hands and prayer for healing. When I heard of my mother's plan, I knew within my heart that the Lord Jesus Christ could heal me, though I questioned my worthiness. But as it says in Romans 10:17, "so faith comes from hearing, and hearing by the word of Christ." I did have faith, and I believe the faith I had came from all that I had learned through the Bible stories I read, and the sermons I had heard in church.

When the day came for this visit, my mother picked me up from Zeals House, which is situated near Mere in Wiltshire. She drove me to the parsonage in the village in Dorset where the Reverend Sharp was resident. This man of God prayed for me to be healed of my illness, and as he prayed I felt as if my body was being touched. As the prayer time drew to a close, the vicar told me to say in my daily prayers that God the Father, and His Son Jesus Christ, were making me better. The vicar's wife then provided a delicious tea with strawberries and cream. After tea my mother took me back to my boarding school, and then went home. That evening I vomited; I have always wondered if that was the fault of the strawberries and cream, or if it was one of the first signs that deliverance was taking place.

For deliverance did come. After I received this prayer for healing, my convulsions became less frequent, and after a few months stopped completely. When the neurologist next saw me, he told my mother that he had fully expected me to get worse and die. My best friend at Zeals House was Deborah, who, like me, suffered from major convulsions, and was seen by the same neurologist. I was moved to another boarding school after my miraculous healing and lost touch with Deborah. A few years later I heard through my mother that Deborah had died.

The boarding school I was moved to next was Hatherop Castle, which is situated in the Cotswolds, in Gloucestershire. It was not easy for me there. It was a much bigger school than Zeals House, and I was very behind in my education. But I knew that the Lord was with me. The miracle of healing that had taken place in my life had a great impact on me. I was greatly strengthened in my faith in the Lord, and He gave me the assurance that He was with me, He knew me, and loved me.

I cannot say when it was that I actually gave my life to the Lord. Having been brought up in a traditional Anglican Church where the message of salvation was never preached, I did not know that I was meant to repent of my sins and ask the Lord Jesus into my heart. However, I can remember one day being up in the attic of my home, totally alone, and singing a hymn with the chorus "come into my heart Lord Jesus, there is room in my heart for

Thee." I sang that chorus with all my heart. I do not know if that day was before or after I was healed. But at that time I understood that the purpose of life was to serve God. I was unaware, then, that there were people in the world who did not believe in God.

As I have said before, I was instructed by my mother to say my prayers before settling down for the night. But I had never been told about having a quiet time with the Lord daily, a time in which I could come before Him in prayer and feed myself from His Word. In Deuteronomy 8:3, it says "man does not live by bread alone, but man lives by everything that proceeds out of the mouth of the Lord." At that time in my life I walked and talked with the Lord. At home, I would go out into the woods alone and talk to the Lord, and whenever we were travelling by train, I would look out of the window, which also inspired me to pray.

Hatherop Castle, however, was not a place where one was encouraged in one's faith, and I am sure that the majority of the pupils did not come from Christian families, nor had they developed a walk with the Lord. We went to the local Anglican Church on Sunday, but at that time it was the custom to do so. There were many nominal Christians in those days.

It was hard for me to build friendships in this school. The girls tended to form cliques, and at times were very catty. The only teachers I can remember are the French teacher, and the maths teacher. The French teacher always reeked of garlic, and the pupils would come with hankies dipped in perfume to survive the class. I can also remember doing exercises where we had to write and recite time and time again, "I am," "you are," etc., in French, but I never really learnt French. When I first arrived at the school after my years of illness, I did not understand decimals. When I asked the maths teacher to explain them, she replied, "you should know that at your age." At that time, I was still kept on anti-convulsion drugs, which I am sure must have dulled my brain a bit.

But the Lord was gracious to me at Hatherop, for He brought about some special experiences that encouraged me in my faith. There was a girl at Hatherop called Mary Kerin. During the Second World War, Dorothy Kerin, who was a mighty woman of God, had adopted her. The Lord had healed Dorothy Kerin from tubercular meningitis, peritonitis, and diabetes when she was twenty-two, after she had been bed-ridden for five years. This miraculous cure restored her to full health overnight. The Lord then anointed her with the gift of healing. She founded "Burswood," a home of healing near Tunbridge Wells in Kent. It is still running today and is now known as Burswood Christian Hospital. The choir at Hatherop Castle was invited to sing at the opening of the chapel at Burswood. Although I was not a member of the choir, the headmistress, Mrs Fyfe (who knew of the miracle of healing that had taken place in my life), made sure to include me in the event. Getting to go to Burswood and meet Dorothy Kerin confirmed to me that Christianity meant more than just going to church.

One night at Hatherop I had a dream. I dreamt that a Jewish girl at the school had stolen butter from the kitchen and was expelled. I informed this Jewish girl (whose name I cannot remember) of my dream, and she told me that it was true, and that she had stolen butter from the kitchen. Until I had told her about my dream she had not had any conviction about what she had done. Thankfully she was not expelled. I was greatly touched that day, because I sensed that God had chosen me to speak to this girl. When I was free I went to the church just outside the school grounds and knelt before the Lord to give thanks to God for speaking through me. At this time I knew little about the gifts of the Spirit such as prophecy, words of knowledge, words of wisdom, or how God spoke to various people in the Old Testament through dreams. The dream and what followed was a learning experience for me.

After three years at Hatherop it was decided that it would be better for me not to take the school exams. At that time, I had a strong desire in my heart to be a nurse and care for the sick, but it looked as if everything was against me. I remember well how I struggled to pack all my belongings into my school trunk at the end of my last term in 1959, and the school matron saying to me that I would never be a nurse if I could not even pack my trunk. I was in a hurry to get my packing done because I was in the school choir and the choir was due to lead the carol service in a local church that evening. I loved singing hymns and carols, and some of the words in the carols I sang came out as prayers for me. One of these was the third verse of "Away In a Manger," which goes "be near me Lord Jesus, I ask Thee to stay close by me for ever and love me I pray."

I clung to the Lord. There were times when I felt like the black sheep of the family. I knew that my parents, with their role in the diplomatic world and their position in high society, would have loved to have me a well-educated daughter of whom they could have been proud. My two sisters were sent to a much more academic school, and my brother to Eton College. But although I felt inferior to my sisters and my brother, and though I felt that I was a burden to my parents, I knew that God would not reject me. I leaned on God as my Father, and Jesus as my Lord and Saviour.

In 1960, my parents sent me to a finishing school in London called "The Monkey Club," named after the three wise monkeys who "see no evil, hear no evil, and speak no evil." The purpose of this school was to teach young ladies how to be part of society. We were taught subjects such as domestic science, comportment, and current affairs. In spite of all the cooking lessons I had, I never felt that I had learned anything. We were also taught dressmaking. I can still remember the one dress I made, but I do not remember ever wearing it. I have a vague memory of two girls, fellow students during my time there. One was from Egypt and the other from Laos. I felt that the "Monkey Club" was just somewhere that my parents felt they could send me in order to occupy me, and fill in the time until I was old enough to leave home. My two sisters were sent to finishing schools in Switzerland. I had no idea what I would do after I left. I continued to go to church on Sundays, but after the service I would return to the "Monkey Club." I did not know any other Christians with whom I could worship and fellowship. It was a very dry time spiritually so I was glad when my time there came to an end.

In my family, it was the custom for children to leave home and live a more independent life when they reached adulthood. Many young women became debutantes for a year when they turned eighteen. A debutante is a young society woman who starts making her formal appearances by going to balls and cocktail parties. Obviously, the monetary cost of a debutante year for parents is very great, with constant expenditures on smart clothes such as ballroom dresses and formal attire that their daughter will need in order to do well. But in the late fifties it was the norm for young women to get married, not go to university. My sister Serena was a debutante during the final year for the debutantes to be presented to the Queen.

She got into Oxford University. When I reached the age when I could have been a debutante, I left home to work as a volunteer in a Church of England Orphanage instead. Due to the effect of my long illness on my life, I did not experience the kind of life that most teenagers do. I did not have friends, and I would not have been ready to go to all the social events. My story was to be very different.

Early Adult Years

My mother was the one who did her utmost to help me find something that I could do with my life. It wasn't an easy task, for I had no school certificates, nor had I developed much in the way of social skills. But she managed to find a Church of England Orphanage in Box, a village near Bath in Somerset, which needed volunteers to help with the babies and toddlers. I accepted the opportunity to work at this place. But when I arrived, I was disappointed to find that the staff were only nominal Christians, and I could not talk to them about the Lord. I loved the children, all of whom were under five years of age, but I still had a longing in my heart to nurse the sick. I can remember one afternoon, while taking some toddlers out for a walk, crying out to God for the opportunity to nurse.

But as it happened, I only worked at this orphanage for eight months, for my wealthy Scottish grandmother (the Granny at Lake) invited me to accompany her on a three-month cruise around the world. I had gotten to know my grandmother better in her later years. I had stayed with her more often at Lake, and many of the old customs of Lake and old society continued there, such as having to change for dinner every evening. When we departed, the year was 1961 and I was nineteen years old. My grandmother was in her seventies, and amazed me by her willingness to join me in shooting the rapids on our visit to Manila. She had invited another friend to accompany her but the friend could not make it, so she took me as her second choice. I certainly learned a great deal about the world, and thankfully, I am a good sailor. On our return journey, as we travelled from Singapore to Aden, the sea was very rough and far fewer people turned up for meals. I thoroughly enjoyed those stormy days.

After returning from the cruise, which had been a great experience, I went to live with my parents in their London flat. I did some voluntary work at the Hospital For Sick Children, in Great Ormond Street, and while I was there, I heard that there was to be a training school for State Enrolled Nurses the following year. The school would take place at the country branch of the London hospital, Tadworth Court, in Surrey. I immediately applied for the course, and to my amazement, I was accepted even though I had no school certificates.

My two years of training as a pupil nurse started in May 1962, first in the classroom, then for periods of time on the wards, and then back in the classroom. At the end of the first year we had a hospital exam, which I failed, but I was allowed to continue because I had done well in the practice of nursing. At the end of the second year there was the state exam; I can remember praying, asking God to guide me as to what I should revise as I prepared for the exam. By God's grace I passed. The questions that came up in the exam concerned exactly the subjects I had revised. There was also a practical assessment to pass, when I was given certain tasks to do under supervision. I can remember only one thing that I did in this assignment, which was to bandage a child's knee.

On the 25th of May, in 1964, my name was entered on the official Roll of Nurses. As my days of training ended, there were no posts available for which I could apply at Tadworth Court, so I went home and started to look for posts that were advertised in nursing magazines. While still at Tadworth Court, I had seen a documentary about the cardiothoracic unit at Great Ormond Street, which had intrigued me. After about three months, much to my surprise, I saw an advertisement for a state-enrolled nurse in the exact unit I had seen in the documentary. At first this seemed too good to be true, but I applied, and was accepted for the post.

While I held this job I lived in the nurse's home at the back of the hospital. It took me a few weeks to get used to the ward routine, but bit-by-bit I adapted and quickly learned many new things. In this ward there were many babies and children of all ages requiring intensive care. Some were nursed on respirators, and others in oxygen tents; many required major heart operations.

During the two years I kept this job, I encountered one baby called James whom I will always remember. James was in need of an operation on his heart, but his lungs were in a bad state, and he was kept on a respirator for a very long time. One day it occurred to me that I could ask the Lord to strengthen James' lungs, and so while I was with him in his cubicle, I went ahead and prayed for him. About two weeks later he came off the respirator. Shortly after that he was operated on, and later was able to be discharged.

Another moment that I will never forget is the day the ward Sister asked me if I would mind caring for a child who had just come back from the operating theatre, having had open heart surgery. I asked the Lord if I should and felt peace about it, so I said yes. The post-operative nursing care was intensive and complex. I had to keep balanced what the child was receiving through intravenous drips and what was being drained out. I was amazed that I could handle such a case with all the mathematical calculations I had to make. I sensed God say to me, "Venetia, you are not stupid."

Nursing in the sixties was very different from what it is today. The nurses wore starched caps, aprons, and collars, and our uniforms were laundered by the hospital. As well as the challenging tasks that we had to do in nursing, there were also the more basic daily chores. On night duty at Great Ormond Street we had to prepare squares of gauze and cotton wool balls, then pack them into drums that were then sent to be sterilised. Needles, syringes, and operating instruments had to be sterilised as well, and the nurses would have to prepare trays with the right instruments for certain procedures. There was no official sterilisation department in those days. Nursing was a vocation, not a degree for which you studied at University.

During my time at Great Ormond Street, I began to build friendships. My first friend was a nursery nurse. She was an Evangelical Christian, and I went with her to St. Paul's, Portman Square, which is an Evangelical Anglican Church. This was a new experience for me, and it was the first time I got to hear the full gospel, and truly learn what it means to be born again. Since then, all the close friendships I have made have been with other Christians. I grew greatly in my faith during the time I attended this church, but it was not until about 1972 that I came to realise that the vicar did not believe that the gifts of the Holy Spirit were for believers today. He believed they were only for the apostles. I could not accept this teaching after the miracle of healing that had taken place in my life. During this time, I found out that Jean Darnel, an American evangelist who prophesied regarding a coming revival in the UK, was to speak at a conference nearby. I was eager to go and so were others from the church, but we were discouraged from attending because Jean Darnel was known to have the gift of tongues. I decided to attend the conference anyway with some friends, and it was then that I started to hear more about being baptised in the Spirit.

After two years on the cardiothoracic unit at Great Ormond Street I felt the need for a change. In 1966 my father had been appointed as the British Ambassador to Bangkok, Thailand, so in September of that year I left my job and went to join my parents at the British Embassy in Bangkok. Thailand has a very different climate and culture to the United Kingdom, and to live in the British Embassy offered a very different style of life to that which I had known. In the Embassy, the bedrooms were air-conditioned and downstairs there were ceiling fans. Most mornings, I had breakfast alone on a balcony, and as I went out of my cool bedroom onto the balcony it was like stepping into a sauna. I was always glad when it rained, for then it cooled down a bit. I picked up a few Thai words, but with the language being tonal it was very difficult to learn.

There were constant cocktail parties in the Embassy, and I remember that as the servants offered drinks there were many requests for whisky nam, (whisky and water) and from that I will always remember the word for "water" in Thai. As the Ambassador's wife, my mother had the primary responsibility for organising all the social events, directing hospitality, and accompanying my father to other diplomatic gatherings. The only grand event I went to was a garden party at the Royal Palace where I shook hands with Queen Sirikit. Prince Philip spent one night at the embassy while I was there.

I did get to travel to other parts of Thailand, and to Phnom Pen, Cambodia. We visited Phnom Pen at the time of a water festival when crowds stood alongside the river to watch a procession of boats. I stood next to Prince Sihanouk, who later became a puppet of the Khmer Rouge. I was also taken to visit Buddhist temples. As beautiful as some of these temples were to behold, I recognised that Buddhism did not blend in anyway with Christianity. At Christmas we went to Pattaya, a seaside resort, where the British Embassy kept a house. I remember feeling sad at the thought that we would not be celebrating Christmas in the usual way. As time went on, I increasingly realised that Embassy life was not for me.

When I first arrived in Thailand, I did voluntary work in a state-run orphanage for the first three months. The standard of care was much lower than any I had ever known before. At feeding time the babies would be put into a cot. No baby had their own cot, and some babies were put together on a large bed. Once the babies were in their cots the carers put their feeding bottles into their mouths and left them to feed alone. I fed as many as I could in my arms, to minister to them the love and affection they needed. Later on I was given the opportunity to do voluntary work in the Children's Hospital in Bangkok. Unfortunately, after a few days in the hospital I became sick. I first went down with bacillary dysentery and then, later, with amoebic dysentery. I was put into a private clinic then, and for me the great blessing was that there was a Christian chaplain there. For the first time in months, I was able to take communion. By March 1967, it was decided to send me home, where it was found that my intestinal system had been compromised. I was not fit to work again until April 1968.

In April 1968 I returned to work in the cardiothoracic unit at Great Ormond Street, but I worked only part time, for I had not yet recovered my full strength. In October 1969 I became ill again. This time I had difficulty walking, and I was admitted to the National Hospital for Nervous Diseases in Queen's Square. After a few weeks I was discharged and told that I would get back to walking at home, but a few weeks later I was readmitted in an even worse state. I eventually learned to walk again with the help of a physiotherapist. 1970 was a year of chronic convalescence. I could walk, slowly, but I had little energy and suffered a lot of pain. I was unable to work, but I managed to get to a lot of Christian conferences and continued to grow in my faith.

In 1971 my father told me that he thought I was living the life of a zombie and suggested that I should find a job. I registered with a nursing agency, but before I started to work I was struck down again with the same sickness and inability to walk. This time I was hospitalised in St Thomas's Hospital for six weeks. I eventually learned to walk yet again, but as I began to convalesce I developed chronic tonsillitis. After taking many antibiotics without any success, I had my tonsils out in December 1971. For a long time, I had needed to take a siesta in the afternoon just to get through the day and I thought this had just become a necessary habit. But after the tonsillectomy I found I no longer needed this rest.

In 1972 I worked voluntarily in a playgroup in North Kensington for six months. (I did not want to take a nursing post until I was sure I had the strength to do so). After six months I decided to look for a new job, as I felt I could not keep going back to the same job. I took a post on the children's ward in the National Heart Hospital. After I began work in my new position, I found that it was not as satisfying as my previous job at Great Ormond Street. Having grown in my faith as well, I found that I had a much greater desire to share the gospel. Some good came to me during my time there. I met a little girl, aged about three, who was in severe heart failure. She had a great impact on me. Every day she sang, "Jesus loves me, this I know, for the Bible tells me so," and as she sang, her face was radiant. After her operation she went to be with the Lord. The radiance of this child's face spoke to me of the joy of the Lord, a joy not dependent on circumstances. She greatly encouraged me in my walk with Him.

After about four months on this job, when I found that I was still not getting any fulfilment, I asked the Lord what He was telling me through this. A picture came to me, of vagabonds and poor people on the street, and I sensed that the Lord was calling me from nursing to work in social work. Wanting to obey the Lord, I handed in my notice and left my job after six months. This was the first time that the Lord had ever spoken to me through picture language. I had never had any teaching on hearing the voice of God.

In January 1973, having left my nursing post, I began to look for a place where I could study social science. I came across Ruskin College, Oxford, where one could study social science without needing a school certificate. I wrote to them, asking for their prospectus. When I read the prospectus I sensed the Lord was saying to me, "Venetia, where you are going will be Christ-centred."

One day during this time, I went to a meeting where Richard Wurmbrandt was the speaker. It was at this gathering that I met a nurse who was working at a rehabilitation centre for drug addicts that was run by a mission called "Life for the World Trust." She informed me that her mission would be holding a conference at the London Bible College in March 1973, and I decided to attend.

Right about this time, I also began to hear other Christians talk about being baptised in the Holy Spirit. One evening I went to a meeting that was held in the basement of Holy Trinity, Brompton Road, where the teaching was on this very subject. At the end of the meeting there was an altar call to go forward to receive the baptism of the Holy Spirit. I did not go forward because I was still not sure about it and I did not want to jump on any bandwagon without being sure it was of the Lord.

Soon after, when I went to the conference at London Bible College, I heard someone ask if the conference was for Spirit-filled Christians. The answer was no; it was for all Christians who were sincere in their faith. Obviously the lectures at this conference were about drug addicts and their rehabilitation, but in the middle of one of these lectures I was suddenly overcome by the most amazing joy. I fell in love with the Lord even more deeply that weekend. At the end of the conference I felt led to work with this mission. I joined them on Friday nights, when they went to streets around Soho in London, meeting drug addicts and inviting them to St Peter's in Vere Street, where they were offered soup, sandwiches, and counsel.

One night, a young woman, badly stoned with drugs, came into St. Peter's and just lay on the floor. She had been incontinent and was soaked. I felt led to go home and bring back a bowl with all that was necessary for personal hygiene, along with a change of clothing. I felt so blessed for having had this opportunity to show God's love and compassion to her.

After a time, I told the Lord that I wanted to serve Him more than one day a week and I applied to work at Northwick Park, the rehabilitation centre of "Life for the World Trust." I was accepted and worked there as a volunteer nurse from August 1973. All who worked there were volunteers, although our board and lodging was provided. The director of this mission was a Baptist minister and it was when I moved to Northwick Park that my connection with St. Paul's in Portman Square drew to a close.

The work in this new community was challenging. It was great to see drug addicts surrender their lives to the Lord and be set free from their addictions, but it was heartbreaking to see those who did not make it. I can remember a very young drug addict who left us. Before long he was back in prison, where he committed suicide by hanging himself in his cell.

But there was a wonderful team of volunteers from many denominational backgrounds who were a joy to know and work with. Although I was a nurse, there was not much nursing to be done, so I helped with the housework and was relied upon to go to the launderette as we did not have the facilities to do laundry at this centre. One of the volunteers who came from the Salvation Army really challenged me by the way she always applied the standard of excellence to the housework she did. She saw housework as a way in which one can worship the Lord. She reminded me of Colossians 3: 22-23, where it says "slaves, in all things obey those who are your masters on earth, not with external service, as those who merely please men, but with sincerity of heart, fearing the Lord. Whatever you do, do your work heartily, as for the Lord rather than for men."

When I first arrived at Northwick Park, I was reading many books about the baptism of the Holy Spirit, and there was one day in my quiet time when I asked the Lord for the baptism. Nothing seemed to happen. I then remembered the time when I was overcome with joy in the midst of the conference at London Bible College, and I wondered if that had been a moment when I received the baptism of the Holy Spirit. I said to the Lord, "If that was the baptism of the Holy Spirit, please confirm it and give me the gift of tongues. I opened my mouth and started to speak in tongues. But then I felt the enemy say, "how do you know that it is not just yourself?" So I asked the Lord to confirm it was from Him. Shortly afterwards I started to sing in tongues. I had never read about this, nor had I ever seen or heard anyone do this.

After I had focused for awhile on the baptism of the Holy Spirit, the Lord started to speak to me about water baptism through teaching tapes. (The Baptist mission had not put any pressure on me to be baptised by immersion.) I had been baptised as a baby, then confirmed when I was at Hatherop Castle, but when I thought of my baptism I sensed that neither of my godparents had been Christians, and Donald Maclean who spied for Russia, was the godfather of one of my sisters. My confirmation had felt to me more like being accepted into the Anglican Church, so I went ahead and was baptised in a Baptist Church in Bewdley, Worcestershire, on Easter Sunday in 1974. A number of ex-drug addicts were also baptised in this baptismal service.

I worked at Northwick Park for nearly three years, until July 1976, but I left when I sensed the Lord saying to me that the season was drawing to an end. When I had first gone to Northwick Park, I had lived at the centre. But later on I had bought a little flat in the nearby village, called Blockley. After I left, I realised that I had not been that well prepared before I had started to work with this mission, and I started to contemplate the idea of going back to nursing and getting a post at the children's hospital in Brighton. I had heard that there were a number of live churches in Brighton where there was good worship and sound teaching.

One afternoon, I went to have tea with my friends, Mike and Rosie Smith, who had been colleagues on the staff at Northwick Park but had left before me. I shared with them what I was thinking of doing, and later on we started to pray for one another. As Rosie prayed for me she received a tongue and an interpretation with it. Through this tongue, the Lord was saying to me, "Venetia, do not make your own plans; I have a plan for your life." So, I waited, and it was during that time that I really learned what it means to wait upon the Lord and be guided by Him.

I appreciated having a time to rest after leaving Northwick Park, but I soon began to feel restless. I remember seeing an advertisement for state-enrolled nurses to receive training in district nursing. This appealed to me, but I knew that it was not God's voice and I did not pursue it. In January 1977 the Lord put a desire in my heart to learn more about intercessory prayer. Some friends of mine passed on the teaching tapes of Joy Dawson and Reona Peterson (now Reona Joly). They were both well-known intercessors. On Reona's tape, it was mentioned that she was based in Switzerland with "Youth With a Mission." This was the first time I had ever heard of YWAM. Later on, I heard that Reona was coming to Brighton to teach in some churches. I had some friends that I had known at Northwick Park, Rita and David League, who lived in Brighton. They kindly offered to have me to stay with them for the conference. I did not realise that this conference was to be a stepping-stone towards my calling. God did indeed have a plan for me and I was about to discover it.

A Call to South America

$\mathscr{A}$ bout ten days before the conference with Reona Peterson, I was having a quiet time when I heard the Lord say clearly to me, "Venetia, I want you to go into Youth with a Mission." When I got to Brighton, I shared this with my friends, Rita and David League. They found this very interesting because they had invited Roger and Doreen Brown (who had also been with us in Life for the World Trust) to come to lunch on the following Sunday. Roger and Doreen were doing the Discipleship Training School at the YWAM base called "Holmstead Manor" in Sussex. This was half an hour by car from Brighton. When I met Roger and Doreen that Sunday, they invited me to visit them at Holmsted Manor the next day, as it was their free day. I also spoke to Reona Peterson at the conference, and told her of my desire to learn more about intercession. She advised me to go through the School of Evangelism at YWAM. This encouraged me even more to accept Roger and Doreen's invitation.

During my resulting visit to Holmsted Manor, I met Lynn Green who was the director for YWAM in England, and was leading the base. When I first met him, he was busy doing carpentry, but he was very friendly and informed me that there would be a Discipleship Training School in April. I was also introduced to Pamela Gregory, who was the base administrator at that time, and through her I obtained an application form for the Discipleship Training School.

I had a very limited knowledge of YWAM. I was walking by faith and not by sight, anticipating that through doing the YWAM School, I would be better prepared to serve the Lord. At that point, I had no idea that God would be calling me into long-term missions work and I had limited knowledge of the vision of YWAM. Soon, I learned more.

I am personally so grateful for YWAM. The mission was founded in 1960 through Loren Cunningham, who responded in obedience to a vision he received from God in 1956. Loren received a vision in which he saw all the continents, with waves crashing onto their shores. The waves then became young people, and it is through this vision that God guided Loren to found Youth With A Mission. If you have any doubts about hearing the voice of God, I recommend Loren Cunningham's book *Is That Really You, God?*

In March I sent my application form to YWAM straight away, applying for the DTS in April. But I did not receive a reply. In May, I attended another conference. This conference included teaching on intercession, and Reona was one of the speakers. While we were all at breakfast, Reona recognised me and asked me what I was doing. I told her that I had applied to do my Discipleship Training School but had not yet heard anything from YWAM. She said, "I know you are to be with us," which to me was a confirmation of my call to go into YWAM. Not long after that I received a letter of acceptance. The Training School was to be held in September 1977, but prior to that there was to be a Summer of Service in August, in Ashford, Kent.

I participated in this Summer of Service and it was the first time in my life that I discovered what it meant to camp in tents. We were given free days on Mondays, and one week a young woman from the town invited me to pass the day with her. She kindly offered to let me have a nice, hot shower. When I returned to camp that night it was pitch dark and I realised that I had forgotten to take a torch with me. It had been raining all that day; I tried to avoid the puddles, but ended up falling into a ditch filled with water up to my waist. That was the end of the shower! The Summer of Service was a wonderful event. We went out to evangelise in the streets during the day, while in the evenings we had meetings in a big marquee that was packed every night. We saw many come to the Lord and many miracles take place. Marriages were restored and healing took place, and on the last night about fifty people were baptised by immersion. Tony Fitzgerald and Lynn Green directed the whole event.

In September of that year I finally went to Holmstead Manor for the Discipleship Training School. It was quite an experience, sleeping on bunk beds in dormitories! I will always remember a girl called Christy, who talked in her sleep and one night said at 3am, "It's time to wake up!" The base was pretty cold but we had a portable gas heater that we carried between the dining room and the lecture room. Many brought their sleeping bags with them to the classroom to keep warm. One of the choruses we often sang was, "I can run like a troop and leap over a wall!" and the actions to this chorus allowed us to jump up and down and keep warm. Despite the discomfort, the teaching was excellent and it was well worth the sacrifice.

The Lord has used YWAM to facilitate the calling of many of His children. In 1960 there were only a few volunteers, where as now in 2013 there are over 18,000. One of the principles of YWAM is to know God and make Him known. To become a part of the YWAM family one is required to do a Discipleship Training School, and the teaching one receives helps one to come to know God, His character, His attributes, and His ways. As we come to know Him more, and experience the joy of fellowship with Him, we should be eager to make Him known.

Another subject that is taught in the DTS is on "hearing the voice of God." As I have said before, I came to hear God's voice without having received any teaching on it before I came to YWAM, but the teaching for me was refreshing and encouraging. Another feature of YWAM life is to practice worship and intercessory prayer. As I have said, it was through my desire to learn about intercessory prayer that God led me into YWAM in the first place.

During my DTS, we gathered in small groups for intercession first thing in the morning, four days a week. Once a week we gathered together for house worship. The presence of the Lord was so evident in these times of worship, and I can remember how the prayers, prophecies, and worship were nearly always on the same theme.

The three main purposes of YWAM are Evangelism, Training, and Mercy Ministries. Under each of these there is a broad spectrum. Concerning training, once one has done the DTS, there are endless other training schools one can do to help prepare for one's calling. During my own time of training with YWAM, I went through four schools; the DTS, the School of Evangelism, the Basic Counselling School, and the Leadership Training School.

Concerning evangelism, the style of evangelism one needs to learn depends on the people group one is to reach. In the middle of my School of Evangelism we went to a town in Sussex where we worked with a church. We were sent out in pairs to knock on doors and to offer Christian books for sale. The first time I went out with my evangelism partner we got a very cold response from all the households we called on. We prayed earnestly for encouragement, asking that we might see people respond positively. We went out a second time, and the first house we visited received us with a warm welcome and we were invited in. The couple in this house happened to be members of the church we were working with. They kindly offered us tea or coffee, which we gratefully accepted as it was midwinter and freezing cold outside. We felt we had better not stay too long for we were meant to be doing evangelism, but as we prepared to leave the couple asked us if we would pray for an elderly lady who had broken her hip. This lady did not know the Lord and I remember praying that the Lord would reveal Himself to her. The next day, we heard that this elderly woman's hip had been healed. The Lord works in mysterious ways "His wonders to perform."

One thing I love about YWAM is that the mission recognizes that all God's children can hear His voice. In John 10:27 it says "My sheep hear My voice, and I know them, and they follow Me." It is important that we personally know our calling, because when one is in missions there will be trials and testing. If one knows one's calling it helps one to resist going home when difficult times arise. It is vital that we learn to walk in obedience and surrender our lives to God, to fulfil His purposes, to live the destiny He has for us.

Another very important teaching one receives in YWAM is that on spiritual warfare. That subject can take more than the usual week allotted to teach, and there are endless books discussing it. One of the major weapons to be used in spiritual warfare is learning to walk in the Holy Spirit and not in the flesh. This is an especially important strength to have when one is living in community. For one thing that Satan hates is unity. He will do all he can to bring about division in teams, among the leadership of a ministry, or wherever possible. In YWAM, one works in teams, and because it is an international/interdenominational mission the teams are often referred to as mottled crews. It can be easy for someone to misinterpret what someone from a different culture is saying.

I remember being at a conference when a woman was offended because an Australian had called her a girl. It is apparently normal in Australia for women to call themselves girls. Some Christians do not realize the power and anointing we have when we keep the unity of the Spirit. A missionary in Colombia told me about a pastor who visited another pastor who was working in a province that was a stronghold of a *guerrilla* group. The visiting pastor preached in his friend's church, and some in the congregation responded and surrendered their lives to the Lord. One of those who surrendered was a guerrilla, and they are usually the archenemies of Christians. When asked why he had given his life to the Lord, he said he had been consulting a witch on how to capture this little town, but the tactics she gave him failed. When he asked the witch why, he was told it was because there was a stronger power. That stronger power was Jesus. Where there is unity the enemy cannot enter in. There was unity between the churches in this little town, and they came together for intercession and prayer. We cannot allow ourselves to get caught up in broken relationships or divisions because we become useless in spiritual warfare. It says in John 13:35 that "by this all men will know that that you are My disciples, if you have love for one another."

After twelve weeks of intensive teaching, all of us in the DTS went to Spain for our outreach. First, we stayed in Madrid, where we divided up into separate groups. I went to Torremolinos for one month. At the end of the school I went home for Christmas. In January 1978 I went back to Holmstead Manor to do the School of Evangelism; nearly all the students who had been on the previous school also came back. During the second school I sensed the Lord was calling me to South America. I had travelled far and wide, but I had never been to South America and did not know much about it. At the end of the school, when they were showing slides of the Philippines and other countries, I knew that South America was for me.

The outreach phase of the School of Evangelism was in Venice, and we stayed at a nearby campsite called "Camping Joly." We were living in tents and as it was only April we all went to bed with our hats and gloves on. We got our fair share of rain, and Camping Joly became like Venice, with little canals running everywhere. There were about four hundred YWAMers who came from all the bases in Europe to take part in this outreach. It was quite a gathering. At mealtimes there were four separate queues for food. Sometimes at lunch marmite (a condiment made from brewer's yeast that can be spread on toast or bread) was served. We were forewarned that marmite was not chocolate, but not everyone got the message! The outreach went very well. I can remember one night when we had an open-air worship meeting very near the Communist Party's offices. At the beginning hecklers threw tomatoes at us, but as we continued to praise the Lord they quietened down and at the end some gave their lives to the Lord.

That was the year of the Mundial (World Cup) in Argentina. The YWAM leaders, who were in the process of buying our first Mercy Ship, the "Anastasis," (which before had been called the "Victoria") thought that they would be able to buy the ship and have it ready to transport all the YWAMers to Argentina for an outreach at

The World Cup. This plan did not work out, and the leaders quickly learned that it takes a good deal longer to buy a ship and make it seaworthy. However, we did have the privilege of having a pizza party onboard the "Victoria" and got to see the old galley (kitchen), where the ovens were covered in thick grease. One could see there was much work to be done.

Derek Prince, an international Bible teacher, spoke at this outreach and he prayed for those who had need of healing. As he prayed for one YWAMer who'd had polio that caused one of her legs to be shorter than the other, her shorter leg grew, after which she threw away her special shoe as it was not needed any more. We always made time for our quiet times every day, and one day during my quiet time the Lord spoke to me through Isaiah 58:6-12:

Is this not the fast which I choose,
To loosen the bonds of wickedness,
To undo the bands of the yoke,
And to let the oppressed go free
And break every yoke?
Is it not to divide your bread with the hungry
And bring the homeless poor into the house;
When you see the naked, to cover him;
And not to hide yourself from your own flesh?
Then your light will break out like the dawn,
And your recovery will speedily spring forth;
And your righteousness will go before you;

The glory of the LORD will be your rear guard.
Then you will call, and the LORD will answer;
You will cry, and He will say, 'Here I am.'
If you remove the yoke from your midst,
The pointing of the finger and speaking wickedness,
And if you give yourself to the hungry
And satisfy the desire of the afflicted,
Then your light will rise in darkness
And your gloom will become like midday.
And the LORD will continually guide you,
And satisfy your desire in scorched places,
And give strength to your bones;
And you will be like a watered garden,
And like a spring of water whose waters do not fail.
Those from among you will rebuild the ancient ruins;
You will raise up the age-old foundations;
And you will be called the repairer of the breach,
The restorer of the streets in which to dwell.

I received this passage as a rhema word, (a rhema word is one verse of Scripture given to one as a confessed word, a creative word, a simple promise) and as I read it I sensed the Lord calling me to mercy ministries.

After the outreach in Venice we returned to England. There was another outreach in Westminster, London in August, and I participated in it. One thing I remember was that I was partnered with Oliver Nyumbu from Zimbabwe. We knocked on British politician Enoch Powell's door, where we were not well received. One afternoon the whole outreach team gathered together and the leaders were calling people forward to receive prophecy. I can remember feeling like a second-class citizen at the time; I thought that such a gift was not for me. But to my great surprise, I was called forward and prophesied over, and through the prophecies my call to South America and mercy ministries was confirmed.

After this event I left YWAM for a few months in order to sell my flat in Blockley, so I could be ready to work fulltime in YWAM. In January 1979 I joined YWAM and moved to the base, "Ifield Hall" near Crawley. I helped to care for the toddlers, and babies of students, and staff in the crèche during the lectures, while I waited for the day when I could leave for South America. There was a special Discipleship Training School running, directed toward those with artistic gifts. Colin and Maureen Harbinson, a married couple who were students at the school, let some of us live in their house in Crawley while they took up residence at Ifield Hall. Colin wrote "Toymaker and Son," a musical drama which became one of the main tools that we used for evangelism. The drama told the story of the Gospel from the Garden of Eden to the resurrection through characters who were toys. The outreach for that DTS was held, once again, in Venice and I participated in it. I remember especially the times during that outreach when "Toymaker and Son" was performed on the streets; the person who played the part of the clockwork doll (one of the toys) was a professional ballerina.

Lynn Green, mentioned earlier, recognised my calling to South America and in October 1979 agreed to let me go to Argentina for a four-month period. I could not speak Spanish at the time, but I managed to understand some of the choruses we sang. One phrase I picked up was "a la mesa", which means, "to the table" and was said at mealtimes. The YWAM base in Buenos Aires was just a small flat. While I was there, a speaker named David Cunningham (no connection to Loren Cunningham) came for a visit. During the time he was there he went to many churches to pray for the sick. I saw a deaf and dumb child being delivered, after which he started to hear and speak. David mobilised us all to pray as well. I remember praying for a person's leg to grow, and it began to grow so quickly that it gave me a fright. During my time there, I also met a very nice couple from Colombia, Angel and Pilar Barrera, who were also at the base for a time. Little did I know that I would be meeting them again in the future, in their own country. I spent a bit longer in Buenos Aires than I had originally planned because of an outreach we did in "Mar del Plata." Mar del Plata means sea of cash or silver, and it seemed to live up to its name. One day, a member of our evangelism team saw some cash floating in the water, and bought a coca cola with it.

I returned to England in February 1980. This time I helped with the créche at Holmstead Manor during the January DTS. I continued that work into the summer, but started to feel that I needed to seek the Lord for my future. One day, Jim Stier, the director of YWAM in Brazil came to speak, and said there was a need for workers in the orphanage in Belo Horizonte. This touched my heart, and it was quickly decided that I would go out in October 1980.

In September a renewal in the Spirit camp was held at Ifield Hall. One of the speakers was Bill Davidson. Bill prophesied over me that the Lord was saying that I had been walking around in circles, but that He would soon lay before me a broad and easy-to-see highway of ministry. In October I left for Brazil. For the first few weeks I studied Portuguese; then there was an emergency in the orphanage and they needed me to start working. Thankfully, babies can understand all languages! But one day in my quiet time, I thought about the prophecy I had received. It occurred to me that what I was doing in Brazil could not be classified as broad, but was more a specialised work. Something more was still to come. After six months I had to leave the country to obtain a renewal for my visa. I did this again three months later and continued to wonder what was ahead.

After I had been in Brazil for eleven months I had to return to England to apply for a long-term visa. I travelled back to England in September 1981, and while I was waiting for my visa I lived with a YWAM family in Crawley. Christmas came and went; yet nothing had happened, so I spent some time with my own family. In January 1982, I returned to Holmstead Manor to help again in the crèche, but it was agreed that they would release me as soon as my visa came through. In the spring, I participated in another outreach in London.

Finally, during a quiet time sometime around March of 1982, I saw the word "Colombia" with a light shining over it. I sensed the Lord was saying that this meant the birthing of a mercy ministry in Colombia. I did wonder sometimes if this new vision was from God, or if it was my own idea. I had started to lose faith that the visa for Brazil would ever come through. But in spite of my doubts, and despite my questioning of the new vision, it did not go away. I continued to pray for both Brazil and Colombia. When July came and I still had not received my visa, I decided to meet with Lynn Green. I told him about the vision I had received concerning Colombia and he told me to write to Colombia and let them know about it. (Wedge and Shirley Almen were the leaders in Colombia at that time, and I had met them during my time in Argentina.)

I wrote to Shirley and had a prompt and exciting reply. Shirley informed me that they had just completed forty days of prayer and fasting on the base in Bogota, during which they had been asking for someone with a vision like my own! She asked me to come as soon as possible. Three weeks later, with a tourist visa, I left for Bogota, Colombia. This was September 1982 and in those days, one could apply for a long-term visa after entering the country on a tourist visa, without having to leave the country. Before I left Holmsted Manor for my departure to Colombia, I was prayed for and commissioned, and I received a prophecy through which the Lord said, "You have the potential of a Gladys Aylward." The life story of Gladys Aylward had both challenged and encouraged me in my earlier years, and the fact that she had been a parlour maid had made me think that maybe God could use me too.

When I first arrived in Bogota, I found myself in a bit of culture shock, for I knew only a few words of Spanish. I first slept in a dormitory with three others, and after a few days there, I found visitors on my bed – Bogota is the capital of the fleas! At times, there was not much food available on the base and we lived mostly on watery soup and bread, or soup with chicken legs floating in it. However, I gradually settled in to life there and in October 1982 a day care centre was opened on the base for children from the poor neighbourhoods nearby. I worked with the under-fives at this centre. At the same time, a woman named Lizbeth was pioneering a new work among the street children. Lizbeth had been one of those involved in M19 (one of the guerrilla groups) before she gave her life to the Lord. At that time, there were no facilities on the base for working with street kids, so we went out to the parks with hot chocolate, offering to cut their hair and do other small things for them in the evenings.

After I had been there for a time, I asked the Lord to make it clear to me in which mercy ministry He wanted me to work. One afternoon, those of us who were working in the day care centre went to visit children in their homes. As I walked into these neighbourhoods I knew the Lord was calling me there. I started to seek the Lord for strategies and ways by which one could reach those neighbourhoods. As I continued to work in the day care centre, I encountered a little boy, Hector Calderon, who was two years old and still in nappies. This child, after he returned home, had been telling his mother, "we must pray before we eat, and we cannot tell lies; it does not please God." His mother, Claudia, came down to find out what it was all about and gave her life to the Lord. I got to know many other families in these neighbourhoods and developed a love for the people.

Invasion Area, Bogota

In December 1984 at our annual YWAM retreat, I shared with the leadership the vision the Lord had given me to work in these neighbourhoods, which are called Invasion Areas. These "invasion areas" are actually shantytowns, where the destitute live in shacks on land that they have commandeered. The leadership prayed for me and God confirmed the vision. The following year, 1985, was a time of preparation for that work. I continued part time with the day care centre, praying and preparing. The Lord called others to the same vision, and soon a team was formed around me. It was decided to call the new ministry "Project Restoration." I spent a lot of time in prayer with the Bartell family, who had recently arrived at the base and were living up in the attic. They were called to work with street kids and were told that they had to be living off the base by June.

It was decided that to start this work in the "invasions" we needed to rent a house near to those neighbourhoods. One day, as we were praying together, the word "signpost" from Jeremiah came up; after that Steven Bartell and I began to walk in that area looking for a house to rent. One house suddenly caught my eye, a home with windows that looked like church windows. So we went to this house and knocked on the door. A lady looked out from a window upstairs and Steven asked her if, by any chance, they were thinking of renting out or selling the house. He received a cold answer, but I felt so strongly that the Lord had called us to come to this particular house that, as we waited by the door, I proclaimed, "ask and it shall be given unto you; seek and you shall find; knock and the door shall be opened unto you." Shortly afterwards, the lady opened the door and invited us in, offering us drinks. Steven asked her the same question again and she said that they were not planning to rent or sell the house, but that a house across the road was up for rent. In other words, this house had acted as a signpost! Immediately, we went to the other house (no sign had been up to indicate that it was for rent) and the lady there agreed to let us rent it.

We moved into that house on the same day the Bartell's had to move off base. We had made it clear to our landlady for what purpose we wanted to rent the house. It took us a few weeks to get the basic furniture we needed. At first, we sat on the floor for our meals, and then Steven made a table. For the first six months, I slept on a mattress on the floor, and then Steven made a homemade bed for me.

At the beginning, my team consisted of the Bartells, Steve and Evie and their children, a Colombian couple named Valentin and Gloria with their children, a Canadian couple named Brad and Lori, a Swedish lady called Korin, and a young Colombian man named Jorge. We started off our new mission by prayer-walking the neighbourhoods around us and looking for any opportunity to help and serve the people. Lori would offer to cut people's hair, and as Evi Bartell was a nurse, we were able to offer a first aid clinic. In the summer of 1985, a missions team came for a short visit from Hawaii, ready to do construction work. As we sought the

Lord on what to do with this gift, we sensed that the family who should receive this blessing should be Claudia Calderon's.

Claudia was the mother of Hector, whom I had gotten to know at the day care centre. She lived in a shack in the rough neighbourhood of Juan 23 with her mother, who had six children, not all by the same father. She had two brothers who were gangsters, both feared in their neighbourhood. When the construction team came, they did a wonderful job in building Claudia a new home. Claudia's brother, Jorge, gave his life to the Lord and was quickly transformed and changed. At this time, another thing we did was to start Bible clubs in the three neighbourhoods

Claudia's New Home

in which we were working. The one I remember best was the one in Louis Alberto Vega. We just went up there and started to worship the Lord out in the open; children came from everywhere and joined us. This became a regular Friday afternoon event. Occasionally, pouring rain made this impossible, but if we couldn't do it, the children always complained.

Louis Alberto Vega was a Communist neighbourhood, and in the beginning we had some small stones thrown at us. But it was just a bit later on that we planted a church in that very neighbourhood; some of the Communist leaders even came to the opening. In January 1986, Valentin had a vision directing him to hold an evangelistic gathering in the neighbourhood of Juan 23. The neighbourhood leaders were open to this, and allowed us to use their community centre. This building had no electric light and a leaking roof, but by God's grace we received the finances we needed to patch up the roof and put lights in as well as seating, even if this mostly consisted of bricks and planks. It was not the cleanest of places but we were grateful.

Valentin had invited a Colombian evangelist to speak and it was amazing to see how God moved that night. There were many who received miraculous healing – one child who had a broken tooth received a new one while another child who could not walk or bend his knee started to walk normally. Another person was delivered from alcoholism and there were many other healings. Others gave their lives to the Lord. It was a beautiful time.

Jorge Mora was the one on my team who had a special gift for working with children; he led the worship and the Bible Clubs. On Halloween, in 1987, he put on a puppet show for the children. We had planned to show it in the open air, but on that day it poured with rain so we had to have it in the house. The house was packed, for to our delight, about ninety children turned up.

By this time we had started to have problems with our landlady; she was becoming unpopular with her neighbours for allowing her house to be used to help people from the poor neighbourhoods. The large gathering on Halloween did not help our case and we knew it was time for a change. As a team, we gathered together to seek the Lord and to ask Him what He was saying in these circumstances. The Lord told us that He would provide us with a property of our own. Before this, I had some contact with the owner of another house nearby and she was willing to let us rent her house short term. We moved there temporarily, and Steve and I began to walk the area again, looking for a house for sale.

Someone from these poor neighbourhoods told us about a big house that was for sale and we managed to make contact with the owners in early 1988. After seeing this house, which had a garden and large grounds in which we could build and expand, we sent out a newsletter to try to raise funds in order to buy the property. In April, I went to Amsterdam for three months to take part in a Leadership Training School. While I was away, Jorge Ballivian from Bolivia, who was part of my team, took over the leadership role. When I was halfway through my school I called to ask whether there had been any response to our newsletter and Jorge informed me that they had received an anonymous gift of $10! On hearing this news I gave thanks to the Lord for the seed that had been sown, however small.

When I returned to Bogota I again asked how things were going with regard to the property. I was told that a taxi driver had reported that it had already been sold. Unfazed, I replied, "we are not going to listen to taxi drivers; we will get back into contact with the owners to find out what is happening." When we visited the house again, we saw that the walls outside the property had been repainted, but that, apparently, was in preparation to sell the property to us. The house was still available, and we came to an agreement to pay for it within two years. Half the finances we needed were received through offerings, and a loan covered the other half. I am thankful to say that the loan was repaid. An interesting part of it all was that at the Leadership School in Amsterdam, every student was required to outline a project idea and make a budget to cover the costs. I did mine in Colombian pesos, and the price of the property we bought turned out to be exactly what I had written in my budget!

We moved into the new property in October 1988. This house was certainly much bigger than either of the two houses we had rented. We needed much more furniture; but God was gracious and bit-by-bit, we got what we needed. The children of the previous owner of the property had used the house for offices. Downstairs were three offices. As you came into the main entrance, on the right was a sitting room that became our reception. Behind that room were two more rooms, which we used as a medical and dental clinic, respectively. We used a covered patio as a dining room, and we had a very large kitchen. Beyond the kitchen was the laundry area, which extended into the back yard. Upstairs were seven bedrooms, as well as a sitting area that looked down on the patio.

The house was in reasonable condition and we felt blessed. We all, on the wonderful

Project Restoration House, Bogota

team that the Lord had given me, looked on this house as God's house. Everyone, spontaneously, helped towards the cost of the upkeep of the house and added little extra things in creative ways. As we settled into the house, I was reminded of the prophecy God had spoken to me in 1981. I recalled his promise of a broad and easy-to-see highway of ministry. I believed that this ministry, Project Restoration, was the fulfilment.

The ministry continued well. One of our teams worked specifically with women, running discipleship groups and teaching them handicrafts.

(Later on, we were able to put up a prefab building for the handicraft workshop.) There was a garage, in which we stored clothing and we were constantly helping poor families with clothing and foodstuff. About this time, Enith Diaz joined our team. She was an auxiliary nurse, but she had operated on people in the jungle. Twice, guerrillas had threatened her with death, but the Lord had graciously preserved her. She took charge of the medical clinic.

I will always remember the day when a woman brought us her two-year-old granddaughter with a severe burn on her left foot. Doctors had said the foot would have to be amputated, but Enith started dressing the burn and, as she dressed it, praying for the Lord to heal it. Enith had a dream one night after that, in which she saw the scar on the child's foot shrink to a much smaller size and the next time the child was brought in, it was exactly as she had seen in her dream! The foot healed completely in a short time and the grandmother gave her life to the Lord. This showed me the importance of ministering to people in both the practical and the spiritual realms.

Obviously, our prime aim was to reach these people with the gospel, but if you are preaching the gospel to the poor and telling them that God loves them, you need to be able to live the gospel and show them God's love in a tangible way. We did not believe we could solve every problem, but we knew how much it meant for us to respect these people and stand with them in times of need. Some were very open to the gospel, while others, whom we called the "give-me" people, wanted only the material goods we offered.

To give an example, one morning as I was walking to our ministry house, I met two ladies, one of whom was carrying a baby hidden under her *ruana* (poncho). The baby was crying. The woman said that she had to get her child to the hospital and wanted money to do so. I told her to bring the baby to our clinic, which she did. When Enith saw the baby there was nothing wrong with it. We were in contact with a doctor in a practice run by the Lions' Club who would treat anyone we sent him free of charge. We offered this woman the opportunity to take her baby to this doctor but she was not at all interested. All she had really wanted was the money.

At times, Enith would visit homes in the neighbourhood, like a health visitor. One day an American nurse from another mission accompanied her. They went to a house that was so filthy that the American nurse passed out because of the stench. There was so much need for teaching these mothers about basic hygiene! Several children came to the clinic because their mothers or grandmothers tended to be drastic in the way they disciplined the children. I remember one little girl who arrived at the door, crying. Because she had broken a plate, her grandmother had hit her with the plate, and this had given her a bad cut. Another boy came because his father had punished him by making him put his hand on a hot iron. It was very hard to make contact with the fathers, because many of them were alcoholics and spent all their money on drink, leaving the women to feed and educate the children on the little they could earn through menial jobs such as washing clothes.

The accepted culture in these neighbourhoods was one of promiscuity, and women often had many children by different fathers. Once a woman had two or three children, the man would often simply abandon them. When the mothers went out to work, they left their older children to care for the younger ones, or even left them locked up in their shack. Children there received very little love and affection from their parents. This made the girls especially very vulnerable, hungry for love and attention from the irresponsible young men who came their way. The whole situation fed the culture of promiscuity so that the evils were continued.

There were times when we went on outreaches to other places. One year we had a School for Mercy Ministries and for the outreach we went to Choco, an area of jungle on the Pacific coast. On this outreach we had students, most of the people from my team, and a few other short-term missionaries who had been recruited through the YWAM base in Hawaii. For this mission, the government lent us two launches. We flew to Bahai Solano, picked up the launches, and travelled down the coast to Pizaro. It was a bit of a bumpy ride, due to the waves, and I remember a fish jumping into the boat.

When we reached Pizaro we were housed in three different places. One was a hotel, while the other two were private homes. Enith was in a house with Raquel and some Americans. Raquel slept in a hammock, while the others slept on the floor. That night, a rat began to crawl over Enith. She shrieked, causing Raquel to fall out of her hammock, landing on top of the Americans. The following day none of them complained, but just laughed. There was such remarkable unity during this whole medical mission! Another addition to our group was an American couple that were short-term missionaries. The husband was a bacteriologist who had brought his mobile laboratory equipment with him. His wife was a surgical nurse. They brought their two daughters with

Health Brigade, Choco, Colombia

them, aged nine and eleven. The two girls played a major part in the mission by playing and singing with the local children.

In Pizaro, we went up-river on our launches to visit hidden communities where we ran medical clinics. While people were waiting to be seen by the doctors, we shared the gospel with them. After five days, we travelled up the coast to a small town called Nuquay, where we stayed in a hotel. While we were there, the owners of the hotel asked us how it was that we were able to love one another and live in such harmony. That made for a wonderful conversation. From Nuquay we continued to go up-river to visit isolated settlements. There was no other way to reach them for there were no roads.

At that time, there was a cholera epidemic. One day, during the final part of our journey up-river, we had to change from our launch to a canoe that brought us in contact with an Indian tribe. These Indians were partially nude and lived in little houses, built on stilts. They used the nearby river for many purposes; they would wash their clothes and bathe in the river, use it for a toilet, as well as for cooking and drinking. Sometimes they used rainwater, for it was a tropical climate where it was very hot and rained often. There were plenty of mosquitoes about. We gave them antibiotics, which they desperately needed and hoped that the cholera might be contained.

One of the most common health problems there was infestation by parasites. Since we had our mobile laboratory with us we were able to examine samples and find out who had that problem. One child's haemoglobin was so low that we had to send her to a hospital down the coast for a blood transfusion. After Nuquay, we went back up to Bahai Solano, and from there went upriver to various other communities. In one town, the people seemed to be very healthy apart from the fact that they all had head lice. So we set up a special clinic there, just for the curing of lice.

After our return to Bogota, we returned to our normal routine. Every morning we gathered for prayer before we went our separate ways throughout the day. As I have mentioned already, we worked with women and helped the poor with clothing, food and medical care. Some in our time specialised in working with children, while Florian ran workshops for men, teaching them carpentry. Other events took place at special times. We received a great deal of support from Sweden, and a Swedish team used to come each year in December and January.

During the rest of the year, they would raise funds for the projects they had planned. One year they put up a number of prefab houses and we were able to house at least four new families. These prefabs provided basic homes, with a good roof, sanitation, two bedrooms, a living room, a kitchen and a bathroom. In one of the families in those new homes, there was a girl named Tatiana, who had completed her training for missions. One year, the Swedish team helped build an extension on a local school; they also built a home and church (the home upstairs and the church downstairs). They also built us a children's playground. Within the grounds of our property we were able to build an auditorium in which we held lectures and seminars, sometimes for YWAM staff and at other times for those in the community. It was exciting to see everything grow and change.

There were many ways in which we could recruit new staff as our ministry grew. Raquel, for example, came from her local church, "Philadelphia," which was very near us, and she helped in reception. After a time she decided she would like to join YWAM officially, and it was arranged for her to do her Discipleship Training School in Cuzco, Peru. Claudia Calderon, the young mother I had met in the day care centre, had so grown in her faith that we decided to send her to the school with Raquel. She went with her two children. When she arrived, she found Cuzco exactly as she had seen in a dream. Once Raquel returned, she became a full-time member of our staff, while Claudia undertook to run the women's workshops and teach them handicrafts. Claudia started to visit other neighbourhoods as well, teaching the same classes to new women.

Four years later, Florian was recruited. His original plan was to help us for three months and then to return to Austria to study architecture. We prayed fervently for him, asking the Lord to give him a vision for missions. During the three months he was with us I noticed that he had a natural friendship with Raquel. Florian decided to join the mission and did his Discipleship Training School in Hawaii. At that time, Raquel wanted to do a School of Graphic Design, and I recommended that she go to Hawaii. While she was there, Florian proposed to her and they married. They now have a family and are the leaders of YWAM in Bogota, and are on the national leadership team.

Another couple on my team were Jorge and Cindy Ballivian. They were very special. Jorge had a natural gift of love and mercy and had so many encounters with people on the streets that it was hard for him to get home. After a few years they felt they needed to take a break and went back to the States, where they took a number of courses with a group that specialises in marriage counselling. On their return, two years later, Jorge started to run marriage seminars and saw many marriages restored, and he trained new leaders to take the same ministry to other places. Within a short time, his ministry had snowballed across the nation.

In his time away, the Lord had also spoken to Jorge about reaching the people of La Ciudad Bolivar, which is a very poor area in the south of Bogota. He went there and walked through every neighbourhood to find out where there were churches so that he could get to know the pastors. He found that all of the churches were isolated from one another. When he met another missionary from a different mission, they began to work together to bring the churches into unity. They began to hold breakfasts and seminars for pastors, to bring the pastors together and strengthen them. This bore wonderful fruit. To give an example of what this area was like, one Thursday night Jorge went to a service in one of the little churches where the Lord was present in an amazing way. But it wasn't until some days later that he found out that among those who had gone forward to receive the Lord, there had been a leader of a guerrilla group whose intention had been to go into this church and kill the pastor!

Another couple were David and Mari Medina. David was our administrator and was a great blessing and help to us. His wife helped especially with hospitality. Bogota was not the calmest of cities. One year, when President Barco was in power, there was a major battle with the drug barons, with bombs going off all over the city. Some were very near to us. David always went out for an early morning jog and had his special route, but on one particular day he sensed the Lord leading him to go another way. Had he run his usual route, he would have been right in the middle of a bomb exploding. Another drama that occurred was when a short-term missionary, while walking down a street, ended up with a bullet in her tennis shoe. Fortunately, she was not hurt at all. We truly saw God's protection.

Going back to myself, I saw my own role as the visionary for the ministry that was called Project Restoration, and I sensed that my responsibility all through this time was to steer the vision according to the way the Lord had spoken. At one time, when

I felt like a jack-of-all-trades and master of none, I sensed the Lord reminding me that the conductor of an orchestra has the knowledge of all the different instruments and through his experience can bring a true unity and harmony. From that, I understood that as the leader of my team, I was responsible to see that each team member could play their part and that as a team we would work together in unity.

I also learned the principle of servant leadership and came to treasure each person on my team; I felt that the Lord had planted some there to prepare them for their future destiny. One example is that Enith is now the Director of YWAM Medellin and has opened a number of homes for street children. One thing I learned was that a visionary generally needs an administrator to help the vision to function in practical ways. I had many detailed responsibilities. Obviously, as a leader, I had the responsibility for my staff and team's personal needs. I also had the responsibility of communications, which was my least favourite task because in those days there were no computers and I constantly had to re-type my letters, or correct my own writing. Another responsibility was the maintenance of all the buildings. I am much more a "people person" and the Lord has given me a special love for the underdogs. I am not good at administration. At one time, I asked the Lord what the difference was between the ministry of Project Restoration and the Street Kids ministry and He gave me a picture of a house that was being flooded, with all the taps left running. I felt He was saying that if you just continue to mop the floor while all the taps are turned on, you can never bring an end to the flood! I sensed that our role was to turn off the taps, in that most street children came from the neighbourhoods in which we were working. Some children were dumped on the streets by parents who couldn't afford to feed them, while others ran away from the harsh treatment they received at home. By ministering to and restoring the families in these poor neighbourhoods, we were helping to reduce the number of children living on the streets. We were turning off the taps.

We received a good deal of help from the Church of the Nations, situated in upper New York State. Bill and Jean Davidson, whom I had met in YWAM in my days at Ifield Hall in England, had left for YWAM Canada in 1979. After a few years there, the Lord had called them to the United States to plant a church there. One year they organised a Christmas play in which they were using me as a role model, and this brought us back into contact. Bill came to Bogota to visit us. After that, from time to time, he would send teams to help us build houses for the poor. Later on, Wendy Luff, a woman who had accompanied them, caught the vision for Colombia. She ended up planting a church in Los Olivos, which is flourishing today with amazing results and has transformed many families. This same church has also opened a children's home, called La Esperanza, or, "the Hope."

Helping the poor families with housing was a great part of our ministry. The first project we completed in this area was the house we built for Claudia's family. Then came the prefab houses, and then the ones that were built by the team from Church of the Nations. Our policy regarding housing was that, when possible, families should help us with the building. Then, at a price they could afford, without interest, they could pay us back and the house would become their own property. We also helped other families to obtain their homes by means of short-term loans. Another project was to help people to find work, or to give them equipment that would enable them to start off in work. Again, as they earned, they could pay us back a small amount. All the money from these repayments was then used for the next house or project.

My heart's desire at this time was to see many come to the Lord through all that we did. I wanted these people to see and feel God's love in our ministry. I looked upon those that we reached as my spiritual children. They are precious to me. Claudia Calderon still keeps in touch with me, and calls me mummy. If the Lord had called me to do so, I could have spent the rest of my life in Colombia.

Three Years in Peru

When the Lord first called me to Colombia, I had no idea how long I would be there. In the original vision I had received for the ministry there, I had also sensed that the Lord would eventually call me on to Peru. In 1994, I began to feel the Lord nudging me toward the realization that my time in Colombia was coming to an end. News started to circulate concerning one of the invasion areas, "Louis Alberto Vega," saying that the neighbourhood was to be demolished and the people to be housed elsewhere. The purpose of this demolition was to clear the land for future development. It was heartbreaking for us to hear this news after all the work we had invested in this neighbourhood. We had planted a church, run a Bible Club, provided a playground, built homes, and personally worked with and helped many people in the neighborhood. But the change was made and the people were moved, and that sad thing is that the last time I visited Bogota, the land had been abandoned and no development had taken place.

Soon after this, the time came when quite a few people in my team were moving on and I felt strongly that my time in Bogota was almost done. I started to seek the Lord for guidance, and sensed the time had come to go to Peru. One Sunday, I accompanied a member of my team to her home church, and a lady, a stranger, prophesied over me. Through this prophecy God confirmed my call to Peru. I had thought that my move to Lima, Peru would be the start of another long-term mercy ministry, and that I would be there for many years. It came as a shock, one day, when I sensed the Lord telling me that I would be there for only three years.

I made contact with YWAM in Peru, where the leader at that time was Betty Mariaca. YWAM did not have a base in Lima, but there was a YWAM base in Cuzco. On the "Project Restoration" team in Bogota we had had Raquel Fabian, a Peruvian, who had gone back to Lima, and I made contact with her. There was also another Peruvian on the base in Bogota, "Gisella," and in 1994 I visited Lima and stayed with Gisella's family. This gave me an opportunity to meet Betty and talk things through. It was decided that when I came the following year, I would stay with a family until I was able to find accommodation.

As my time in Bogota drew to an end, Jorge Ballivan from Bolivia took over the leadership of Project Restoration. There was a deep cost to me in moving on. I was grieved to leave my team behind, as well as to part with the many Colombian people whose lives had been touched – especially Claudia. Furthermore, Colombia had become my home. But the Lord gives one grace for a season, and when that season comes to a close, one has to move on in obedience.

In February 1995 I departed for Peru. I first stayed with cousins of Gisella, and after a few weeks, moved to Gisella's home. Her mother was a widow who was the pastor to a church in her own house. Most of those who came to this church were ex-Catholics who had been part of a Catholic charismatic movement that was rejected by the Church because of the movement of the Spirit. Gisella's mother, Charito, was an ex-Catholic herself.

Betty Mariaca was running the Discipleship Training Schools. During the teaching periods, she would hire the mission centre of the Swiss Mission just outside Lima. For each outreach, the school travelled to other locations. During the time I stayed with Charito, I got to know some Peruvian people. One was Pastor Eduardo Garcia, whose wife, Juanita, was an Australian. This couple, with their two children, were leasing a big house, but they were not using the top floor and it was agreed that they would sublet the top floor to me. On the top floor there were two bedrooms, a bathroom, a kitchen and a small living room. I moved to this flat after about six weeks. As the time drew near for the next DTS, two other YWAMers joined me in my little flat. One was Clarissa Jacques, from Switzerland, and the other was Rosa Rocha from Mexico, both of whom came to help with the school. While the DTS was running they were often away from the flat, but there were seasons when we were together; we had wonderful friendships.

After a few weeks in Lima, I made contact with Raquel Fabian, who at that time was working with her church in a very poor neighbourhood called Delicias De Villas, in the district of Chorillos. It had been arranged for me to meet her in this place and, by God's grace, I managed to find my way there in a mini-bus. Many of the buses had broken windscreens – not the highest class of transport!

This was a very poor neighbourhood, with many people living in shacks, very similar to what I had known in Bogota. Raquel's church had meetings, sharing the Gospel with the

Baptism, Peru

poor families, and also helping them in practical ways. Her church was an evangelical church that did not move in the gifts of the Spirit, but for me it was a stepping-stone to greater things.

There were many conferences taking place in Lima and many of them focused on spiritual warfare. Anna Mendes, a well known woman of God in Latin America, was the speaker at one of those conferences. After attending it, on a Sunday, during the time of worship in the house church, God brought Exodus 14:15 to my mind: "then the Lord said to Moses, 'Why are you crying out to me? Tell the sons of Israel to go forward.'" I sensed the Lord saying that we needed to step forward and begin to engage in spiritual warfare in the poor neighbourhood where I was working.

Charito received the same message and felt the same as I, so it was decided that we would go away together to walk and prepare for a day of spiritual warfare. We began our day near Raquel's church in a valley, and from there we started to walk up the hillside. We found a cross that was covered with symbols of death. Although we were supposed to be preparing for a day of spiritual warfare, we started to pray around this cross and then walked on. In that area it was desert and there were no proper roads. A car started coming towards us, shifting the sand, so we took a turning to the right. We came to a house that looked a little different from the other houses. A man was standing outside. As we talked with him, we learned that he was the highest authority over this area. He began to tell us its history. What we heard so excited Charito that when she had some New Zealanders come to stay the following weekend, she decided to take them to see this cross before going on to another place where she was planning to buy some land for a retreat centre.

When we got back to the cross, this time we noticed a building nearby which happened to be a Christian school. The founder of the school had seen us standing by the cross and thought we must be missionaries; she came out and invited us into the school. The moment I met this woman, Sara Llamoca, my spirit bonded with her. She invited us up to the open patio, where, during the break, the children came out and performed some amazing choreography taught them by Sara. Sara had done a course with King's Kids, which had been taught by Dale Kaufman, the King's Kids founder. From that day, I felt a sense of purpose, for I believe that the Lord's intent for this time was for me to be a support to Sara.

Sara is an amazing woman of God who came from a very poor background. Her mother was widowed very young and was left to care for ten children. All the children, as well as going to school, had to do their share of work to help the family. Sara had trained to be a teacher. At first she went out to the provinces to teach, and then the Lord called her back to Lima and told her to start a school for

Christian School, Peru

poor children there. She began teaching in a classroom made of straw and cardboard, but the Lord brought her into contact with a Swiss mission and, thanks to them, she now has a three-storey building. Many of those who work with her are members of her own family, some of whom have done a Discipleship Training School with YWAM.

She also founded a church, using the main assembly hall of the school for the services. The children in her school were aged from preschool right up to secondary school age, and these children were intentionally discipled in the ways of the Lord. Sara told me of an incident in a class when a student began to curse the teacher. The teacher sensed that the voice was not the child's own voice, so she told the other children to worship the Lord. Within a short time the child who had been swearing fell to the ground and was delivered.

Because of Sara's training with King's Kids, she held youth camps for youths and children during the summer holidays and with the other staff and children at the school, often went out evangelising in the streets. I had the privilege of working with her for two years, helping to run these camps.

During the camps, the classrooms were turned into dormitories, and one became a dining room. For the first youth camp, we had many local pastors helping out as well. Both Sara and I were invited to be part of the fraternity of pastors in this area.

During the second youth camp, Cristo Manuel from YWAM Bogota came and taught on spiritual warfare. One morning, as he was teaching, a gang leader, who was also a drug dealer, barged in with the intention of interrupting the teaching. But there was such an amazing presence of the Lord that he fell on his knees and gave his life to Jesus! I remember especially from this time how easy it was to evangelise. I shared the gospel with many taxi drivers; one taxi driver, after arriving at the school, stayed and spent half an hour with the pastor and gave his life to the Lord. The church began to grow quickly, mainly through the transformed lives of the children who then reached their parents.

Many of the children who came to the school were given breakfast when they arrived for classes in the morning, as they had not been fed at home. Some children came from such poor homes that their parents could not afford to look after them and the Lord started to lay a burden on Sara's heart to open a home for these needy children. In 1997, Sara decided that she needed a car. I travelled with her by bus down to Tacna, where one could buy cars at a better price. By God's grace, we were able to get one. On our journey home the car was "baptised" as we made our way through terrible floods.

After this journey, with the car issue settled, we started to search for land on which we could build a home for the children. Land around Lima was expensive so we decided to go to the area of Juan de Lions, which is where Charito had bought land to develop a retreat centre. By God's grace, we found land there at a cheap price. The land there is desert, but becomes very fertile when it is watered. We met a man who showed us his own irrigated and fertile land; it was amazing. Many things grew plentifully on it, just like in Israel.

After this visit we began negotiations to buy the land. I felt called to leave Peru before the orphanage was completed. But by the time I left Peru in 1998, the property had been purchased, a wall had been built around it, and there was one small house on the site. In 2000 I returned with a team made up of people from YWAM and people from a London

Children's Home, Peru - Residence   *Children's Home, Peru - School Room*

church. The leader of the team was Bertin Hermo of YWAM London. We stayed at the orphanage, which had been built by then, and worked with Sara for two weeks.

Called Home to Intercede

I arrived home in 1998 after three years in Peru. Coming home to England after my time there was a much worse culture shock for me than what I had experienced when I first went to South America. It was hard for me to find my own nation in such a secular, and backslidden state compared with what it had been when I left in 1982. I knew clearly, then, that the Lord had called me home to intercede for my nation. The Lord had spoken to me about this during my time in Lima, especially at those conferences on spiritual warfare. He also spoke to me directly about this during a retreat held at my little church, when Anna Mendes had been our guest speaker. She had prophesied over me concerning my call to return home and pray for my nation.

On returning to England, I moved to Harpenden, which is where all those whom I had known at

Holmstead Manor had moved to while I was in South America. I stayed on the base for the first three months and then, by God's grace, was able to buy my own house. I did not have a specific role or official title during my time there, but I was very involved in intercession, and I went to many other gatherings of intercessors in London.

In 2003, during one of their community meetings, a YWAMer came and prophesied over me, saying that the Lord had not finished with me. After this, I started to seek the Lord as to what He had for me. As I considered staying at Harpenden, the Lord gave me no peace about it. Suddenly, Scotland came into my mind. I wondered what this meant. Following the idea of Scotland, I found that whenever I turned on the television or the radio or met with friends, Scotland was always the subject that came up. I began to feel that the Lord was calling me there, so I asked the Lord for confirmation.

My specific prayer was that the Lord would confirm this new direction by giving me contact with one of the leaders of the School of Intercessory Prayer at the YWAM Seamill Centre on the west coast of Scotland. This was a school that I had considered attending some day. After praying for that confirmation, I shared with a special friend what I felt the Lord to be saying, and told her of my specific request. She then informed me that Inger Olsen, one of the leaders of the Seamill Centre, was coming the next night. To me, that was exactly the confirmation I desired. I was able to meet Inger and we had a lovely talk and time. I felt clearly now that the Lord was calling me to Scotland, not necessarily to YWAM alone, but also to link up with many other intercessory groups already active in Scotland. I applied to do the School of Intercessory Prayer in 2004. When I got my acceptence, I put my Harpenden house on the market. By this time my finances had begun to feel a bit tight, but fortunately I ended up by selling my house for twice the value that I had paid for it.

When I visited the Seamill Centre I met with Inger again. I found, much to my surprise, that she only had a very small room on the base so I invited her to live with me once I had a house. By God's grace, I was able to buy a little bungalow that was ten minutes' walk from the base. This bungalow became mine on 5th March 2004. This gave me time to get settled before the school started and Inger moved in with me a month later. The school strengthened me in the gift of intercession, but the part I enjoyed most was the outreach, when we went to the Outer Hebrides and took water from there as a symbol of water from the well of Revival. We took it with us up to Thurso in the north of Scotland and we did many prophetic acts.

All of us believed then and now that the Lord will, in His time, cause a revival to start in the north and spread to England and Europe, as spoken in the prophecy of Jean Darnell. After we left Thurso, we travelled south as far as Hadrian's Wall and then began our journey home. As we drove along we were amazed to see rainbow after rainbow out of our windows.

After the school I went to a "Lydia" conference where I met Sue Elder. I found out that both Sue and her husband Tom were living in West Kilbride and apparently attending the same church that I was – St. Andrews. After meeting at the conference, Sue and I began to meet weekly for a time of prayer. Tom, Sue, and I had felt a real hunger for deeper teaching of the Word of God during our time at St. Andrews. In 2005, I was informed of the life in a nearby church called the High Kirk in Stevenston. The first time I visited this church, the pastor, Rev. Scott Cameron, greeted me with open arms. I saw that he had a deep passion for Christ, and was truly anointed to preach and teach the Word of God. At Easter, Tom and Sue came with me to the Passion Week at the High Kirk. Kenny Borthwick was the speaker. He too, we found, was a mighty man of God, and after that week, we all began to regularly attend the High Kirk.

During this time, I also began to go to many other conferences of intercessors in Scotland, so that I would be aware of the prayer and ministry happening in that country. I strongly believe that when one moves to a new place for ministry, one needs to invest time in building relationships and getting to know the culture.

But in March 2005, my health took a bad turn. I started to suffer from blackouts, which meant I had to give up driving. The following year, when things seemed to be no better, I took a retreat so that I could seek the Lord to hear what He was speaking into my life during that confusing time. The retreat centre I chose was called "The Bield," near Perth. It is a lovely place. As I walked through the grounds and sought the Lord, there were lots of free-range chickens running about. What should the Lord then say to me but "Venetia, you are a free-range chicken!"

I then got a picture of battery (nesting) hens in their cages and sensed that the Lord was speaking to me about YWAM. The whole purpose of YWAM is to train Christians in such a way that they will grow spiritually much faster than if they were simply members of churches. During this training, they learn how to live in community. In the same way, battery hens are bred and fed so that they will grow quickly – you could even say that they 'live in community.' But after having been a full-time YWAMer for 21 years, I sensed that God was saying He wanted to release me to walk amongst the body of Christ in a free-range capacity. I sensed that He would use me then to bring about links in the relationships of other believers and those in ministry. One of my greatest dreams is to see unity in the body of Christ.

During this retreat I also sensed that the Lord was showing me Kilwinning, a small town near my home, as a railway junction. This is true of the actual town, for there are four trains to Glasgow, two trains to Ayr, and one to West Kilbride that pass through Kilwinning every hour. It is a place of connection, just as I was to become a person of connection, and I sensed the Lord prompting me to move to Kilwinning.

In March 2006, the Lord also called Tom and Sue Elder to move to Kilwinning, which is much nearer to Stevenston and the High Kirk than West Kilbride. When I returned from my retreat and began to plan for my move, I realised that I would have to inform Inger my plans to move on. This was painful, for we had lived together for over two years. But I knew it was the right path, and when I shared the details of my house with those I knew in the National Office, I received an offer on my house the very same day! A few weeks later, the buyers, Andy and Yvonne Hall, shared with me what they could offer for my house and I accepted their offer. When they came, they brought with them the papers of my new little house in Kilwinning and I knew that God was truly in this move. The Lord provided miraculously for Inger to have her own flat and I was soon settled.

Now, as I write, my house in Kilwinning is only ten minutes walk from my friends Tom and Sue Elder, and ten minutes walk from the train station. Soon after my move to Kilwinning, I began to go regularly to the House of Prayer in Troon, a meeting held on Tuesday mornings. Through this, God provided me with wonderful friends, the McKies, who also live in Kilwinning and who always gave me a lift to the House of Prayer during the time I was without a car.

In 2008 my health improved, and in March 2009, I was able to drive again. The House of Prayer at the Lighthouse church closed down, and the High Kirk became my main focus. Since I first started going to the High Kirk I have faithfully attended the Revival Meeting on Friday evenings in the Manse. It is a time of worship, teaching of God's Word, prayer, and ministry. At this gathering, I have always known an amazing presence of the Lord. After Easter in 2011, we at the High Kirk began to have informal gathering on Sunday evenings. For some time now have held this meeting in the Hayocks Community Centre on the first Sunday of the month. The Hayocks is a neighbourhood in Stevenston which is a part of the High Kirk Parish, and it is the prime area we are aiming to reach with the Gospel.

I have also been part of the Healing Rooms team in the Three Towns. (The Three Towns is the name for an area including the towns of Stevenston, Saltcoats, and Ardrossan). The team members are from various churches in the area and I have loved being part of the healing work. One miracle of healing that I will always remember is when the Lord healed a schoolgirl who had arthritis in her hands. When she first came, she could not open her hands, but as we prayed she suddenly started to open and close them, saying to her father "look daddy!"

I have also interceded a great deal for another prophetic evangelism movement called "Light and Life." This movement is interdenominational and they hold large spiritual gatherings in big hotels and small ones. The gatherings are called Light and Life Fairs, and at every one I have attended, people have given their lives to the Lord, and amazing healings have taken place.

In all of the work and prayer I have done, I am aware that the Spirit is at work in Scotland. Great things are happening here, but I believe that what we have seen so far is only a trickle of what is to come. I live here and pray, and look forward to what is ahead. I feel that there is great potential nearby.

Within the Three Towns area in North Ayrshire, there are many needy people. There is a high level of unemployment, problem families, gangs, drug addicts and very lonely people. The main shopping street in Saltcoats is full of pound shops and charity shops. One could call this area a backwater place, a forgotten place. But I believe we will see transformation right amidst it. Nathaniel, the disciple of Jesus, wondered if "any good thing could come out of Nazareth," John 1:46. I am sure there are people who think the same about the Three Towns, but in the nineteenth century (about 1860), there was an amazing revival in North Ayrshire. This revival reached many children, and I believe that something great can happen here again.

As I draw near the end of my story and reflect on the way the Lord has allowed me to become involved with people from different levels of society, I often think of Moses. He was brought up in Pharaoh's household, but he knew his true identity was with the Hebrews. He was willing to give up the luxuries of living in a palace, and to live in the wilderness of Midian, a foreign land, caring for sheep for forty years. He met with God at the burning bush, and God called him to go to Pharaoh to bring His people out of Egypt.

Like Moses, I was born into a privileged family, but I knew that my identity could only be found in Christ. I too began life in a very different place from where the Lord has now led me, but like Moses, I have followed God. Nothing gives me greater joy than to serve the Lord in whatever way I may and to see His name glorified. My brother Henry inherited Hatch House and the estate, and my sister Serena and her husband have a lovely Cotswold house. But I am content with my little house in a Scottish town. For me, a large property would be a white elephant that could restrict my freedom to serve the Lord, and to go where He asks me to go.

As I end this book, I want my reader to know that God can start to prepare us for His calling before we know anything about it. What the enemy Satan means for evil, the hard things or grievous things in our lives, God can turn around for good. In Romans 8:28 it says that, "we know that God causes all things to work together for good to those who love God, to those who are called according to His purpose."

The sickness I bore as a child taught me what it meant to be somebody who is not respected, who has little sense of self-worth. Only in my faith, as I grew to know how deeply God loves me, did I come to find my true identity and worth. When I worked in Colombia and Peru amongst the poor, people who greatly lacked a sense of self-worth, I could identify with them. God gave me a love for these people, and made me aware how precious each one of them was to Him.

In many parts of the world the poor are looked upon as the scum of the earth. In my childhood, it never occurred to me that God would call me as a missionary to work among the poor. But it became one of my great blessings to see the change in the lives and faces of those who gave their lives to the Lord, and came to understand their true identity in Jesus. It says in James 2:5, "listen my beloved brethren: did not God choose the poor of this world to be rich in faith, and heirs of the kingdom which He promised to those who love Him?"

I have heard it said that before I became ill I was the brightest of the children. I don't know if this is true or not, but even if I was average and had been given a good education, I could have reached a good position in a profession such as nursing. But if I had become self-sufficient I may never have come to recognise my need of the Lord or have worked with the people and places to which he led me. When I was in Bogota, Colombia, a team of professional people came out to help us for a few weeks. I got the impression that these people wanted to use their professional gifts to serve God. It is right that we should use our gifts, but at the same time we must recognize our deep and ceaseless need, regardless of our intelligence or skill, to depend upon the Lord.

There are those who have not fully surrendered their lives to the Lord. Many know of Him but have not come to an intimate relationship with Him. They do not know what it means to hear His voice. My own life helped me to know my need for God, and I am so thankful. Christianity is just not knowing about God, but coming to know God Himself, and then from that love, to make Him known. We all need to grow in our relationship with God; we must constantly seek a living faith. And if we hear God speak to us, telling us to go somewhere new or do something difficult, we must obey and step out in faith.

Even now, after years of knowing the Lord, I hunger after God's Word. It is through His Word that God renews our minds and sets us free from the mindset of the world. In Romans 12:2 it says "and do not be conformed to this world, but be transformed by the renewing of your mind." I can barely express how much it means to me to know that I have been saved by grace through faith. I can identify with Paul when he says in Philippians 3:8 that "more than that, I count all things to be loss in view of the surpassing value of knowing Christ Jesus my Lord."

In the end, what the story of my life comes down to is that I have decided to follow Jesus. Jesus told His disciples to "follow Me." There is a cost to being a Christian, but it is worth the price. I have learned this in every turn and new adventure of my life. And as I go onward, I believe that I will see a revival with signs and wonders. As I wait and pray, I believe with all of my heart that many will come to the Lord.

I hope your own faith has been strengthened by this story. To those who have read this short narrative of my life, the story of my journey with the Lord, I would just like to say that God does not have favourites. God has a clear calling for all of His children. I found this in my own life and I believe it to be true of yours. He loves us with an everlasting love. Follow Him.

Lightning Source UK Ltd.
Milton Keynes UK ·
UKOW05f1914171113

221221UK00001B/76/P